Sweet
FA

This edition published in the UK in 2003 exclusively for

WHSmith Limited
Greenbridge Road
Swindon SN3 3LD
www.WHSmith.co.uk

Created by Essential Works
168a Camden Street
London NW1 9PT

The author and publishers have made every reasonable
effort to contact all copyright holders. Any errors that
may have occurred are inadvertent and anyone who for
any reason has not been contacted is invited to write to
the publishers so that a full acknowledgement may be
made in subsequent editions of this work.

A catalogue record for this book is available from the
British Library.

ISBN: 0 9545493 1 7

Printed and bound in Singapore

Sweet FA

Martin Horsfield

I'M A CELEBRITY... GET ME A SEASON TICKET

Fulham have had their share of celebrity fans over the years, from The Sweeney hardman Dennis Waterman to Hollywood's favourite fop Hugh Grant. One who got away was Michael Jackson, guest of chairman Mohammed Al Fayed at a match versus Wigan Athletic in 1997. It obviously wasn't the right type of thriller for the baby-dangling King of Pop, who left at half-time. Craven Cottage became a 'neverland' for Jackson as, shortly afterwards, he joined his chum Uri Geller on the board at Exeter City. Geller claimed to be behind Scotland's Gary MacAllister missing a penalty against England in Euro '96 by making the ball move. Perhaps he is responsible for another football trick – Exeter vanished from the football league at the end of last season.

Kid: 'How would you describe that first half, Michael?'
Jacko: 'Bad!'

CRIMINAL RECORDS

While the combined vocal power and heart-throb status of England's 1970 World Cup Squad scored a Number One record with *Back Home*, these days the cream of British pop can't conspire to give England top spot. Most ignominious was *Top Of The World*, the FA's official World Cup song from 1998, which boasted Echo & The Bunnymen's Ian McCulloch crooning alongside The Smiths' Johnny Marr and sundry All Saints and Spice Girls. It limped to Number nine, knocked into a cocked hat by the more tongue-in-cheek *Vindaloo* by Fat Les. For once, however, the FA were quick to spot the error of their ways. They roped in Fat Les to pen their anthem for Euro 2000.

Fat Les curried favour
with the FA

GET YER KIT OFF

The rot set in the 1980s with pin stripes and contra shadowing (whatever that was) as football clubs investigated ways to make their shirts stand out better under floodlights and on TV. Since then, football shirt design has been getting ever more ambitious with unfortunate experiments in silver (Manchester United), gold (Arsenal), and truly laughable tiger stripes (Hull City). On the international stage, Croatia's red, chequered shirts look more akin to something you'd see waved at the end of a Grand Prix, while the jerseys worn by Mexican keeper Jorge Campos genuinely do blur the line between football shirt and jester's outfit.

SAY WHAT?

A burglary was recently committed at Sunderland's ground and the entire contents of the trophy room were stolen. Police are looking for a man with a red and white carpet.

Jorge Campos' attempts at dazzling the opposition strikers with his shirt pay off

Rooney: 'Oh, here's that tenner you lent me, Michael'

MY NAME IS...

You'd have thought that the influx of continental names into the game would have posed the most problems for shirt manufacturers, all of whom now offer to put our idols' names on the back of replica kits. However, the biggest headache was caused by the sudden ascent to fame of Everton's Wayne Rooney. After his excellent debut for England, demand for England shirts with 'Rooney' across the back soared. The only problem was that sports retailers didn't have enough letter Ys to keep up with demand – they wised up quickly!

INJURED PRIDE

For every career-threatening injury that's the result of a death-or-glory tackle, there's a more embarrassing reason why our football favourites sometimes don't make the first XI. Kidderminster Harriers captain Sean Flynn suffered a broken nose and bruised toes after tripping over his son's toy cars, Barnsley's Darren Barnard slipped in a puddle of his puppy's wee, suffering knee ligament damage, and Portsmouth's John Durnin crashed his golf buggy during a round with team-mate Alan McLoughlin while admiring the view rather than looking where he was going and dislocated his elbow, putting him out of the game for six weeks. Even England keeper David Seaman has had to pen Sven an embarrassing sicknote. His injury? A back strain, from reaching for the remote control to set the video for *Coronation Street*.

Darren Barnard considers the ignominy of missing a match after slipping in his puppy's wee

Wimbledon FC: for some reason
teams didn't relish a visit

UNGENTLEMANLY CONDUCT

The masters at attempting to gain a psychological advantage were the 'Crazy Gang' of Wimbledon FC, who would rile the opposition by playing loud music in the adjoining dressing room or – allegedly – fixing the showers at their ground to run at Arctic temperatures. Perhaps the most celebrated example of dirty tricks, though, came before the 2001 Germany versus England World Cup Qualifier. First the German FA allocated our boys a hotel situated next to a rowdy beer hall. Then, in a revenge strike, *The Sun* newspaper sent an oompah band to play all night outside the German base. Their headline? 'The Oompah Strikes Back!'

Catalina's nightmares were becoming ever more vivid

MASCOTS BEHAVING BADLY

As if the boys in blue weren't busy enough, the last few years have seen them having to take a menagerie of furry and feathered creatures off for questioning – but none of the culprits have done any bird yet. The most persistent offender among football mascots is Swansea's Cyril The Swan who was fined £1,000 for running onto the pitch and charged with bringing the game into disrepute. Cyril's rival, Bartley the Cardiff City Bluebird, also made headlines for landing a punch on Bury FC's Robbie The Bobbie, while Rochdale's Desmond The Dragon was led away by police after a set-to with Halifax Town's Freddie The Fox.

BLESS THIS STADIUM

When results aren't going the right way, and all the excuses have been exhausted, it's not uncommon for football managers to blame the spirits (no, not whisky). Oxford United employed the Bishop of Oxford to bless their new Kassam Stadium after gypsies evicted from the site were thought to have put a curse on it. Southampton FC opted for an even more ancient religious ritual after weeks turned to months without a win at the St. Mary's stadium. They enlisted a Pagan healer called 'Dragonoak' to counteract any bad vibes that may have been caused by opting to build the main stand over an ancient burial ground. Some, however, have opted for a cheaper – and simpler – approach. When he was manager of Birmingham, Barry Fry peed in all four corners of St. Andrews in an attempt to lift their ancient gypsy curse.

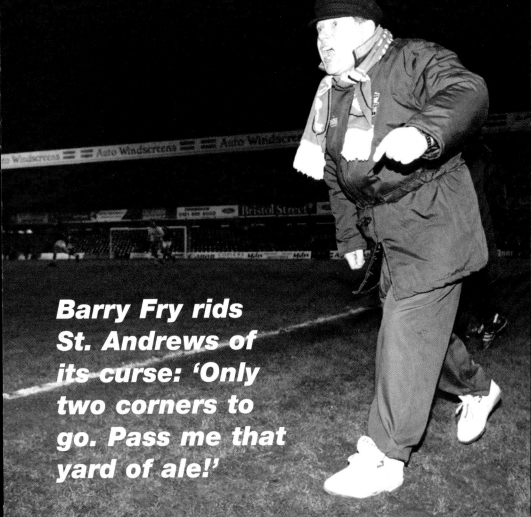

Barry Fry rids St. Andrews of its curse: 'Only two corners to go. Pass me that yard of ale!'

**Health warning:
this pie is about
to bite back**

THE UPPER CRUST

The answer to that perennial terrace chant aimed at players and fans of a more well-rounded stature – 'Who ate all the pies?' – can now be revealed. It was Everton. During the course of the 1999/2000 season, Everton devotees munched their way through a staggering 113,118 hot pies. And, as if to back up Roy Keane's infamous complaints about the prawn sandwich contingent among Manchester United's fan base, this was one league table in which they finished bottom, with only 1.04 per cent of their crowd opting for any kind of pastry product on a Saturday.

SPOT OF BOTHER

It's fairly common for fans behind the goal to whistle, boo and generally wave their arms around a bit in a bid to put off opposition players lining up a spot-kick, but their efforts rarely make a difference. More effective by far were the tactics of one female fan of Somerset amateur team, Wookey FC. The woman in question repeatedly lifted her shirt to bare her chest at the opposition's penalty takers. She caused three consecutive Norton Hill Rangers to boob their shots and so her beloved Wookey won Somerset's Morland Challenge Cup final 3-2 on penalties, following a 0-0 draw.

Ever wondered why Brazil are so good at penalty shoot-outs?

RELEGATION DOGFIGHT

'Even Men With Steel Hearts Love To See A Dog On The Pitch' sang Tranmere-obsessed indie band Half Man Half Biscuit in 1995, although Lincoln City diehards might disagree. The Imps could have been spared relegation to the Conference had it not been for a canine intervention. Also in the relegation battle that afternoon were Torquay United, who looked doomed when they went 2-1 down at home to Crewe. Enter Bryn the police dog, who slipped his handler and promptly sunk his teeth into Torquay defender Jim McNicol. The referee had no option but to add four minutes' injury time to compensate for McNicol's injury, during which The Gulls scored a late equaliser condemning Lincoln to the dreaded drop.

MATCH ABANDONED

Never mind rain, snow or fog: you get a better class of excuse for football matches being abandoned in Iran. A game between Kar-O-Technic and Iran-Sport in December 2000 had to be called off after a stray dog attacked a linesman. The players ran for their lives, but the unfortunate official wasn't quick enough and – with the help of fans by the touchline – had to hold the dog at bay with his flag for 20 minutes. After his ordeal, he was too traumatised to officiate. Besides, there wasn't much left of his flag.

SAY WHAT?

Q: What have Rangers and a three-pin plug got in common?
A: They're both useless in Europe.

Another successful Rangers European campaign

TOUPEE OR NOT TOUPEE

An evergreen feature in early football fanzines was a nostalgic look at follically challenged footballers. It seemed there was a spell in the 1970s when it was mandatory for every team to field a baldie. The most celebrated, of course, was Bobby Charlton who perfected a special cover-up hairstyle – the comb over, as also modelled by the man in the photo booth in those cigar adverts. No such contingencies for Bulgarian goalkeeper Borislav 'Bobby' Mikhailov, however. He proudly earned over 100 caps for Bulgaria in the 1990s, most of which he placed over his perfectly positioned wig.

SACK THE BOARD

Football chairmen are in danger of becoming as infamous as some of their players. Peter Risdale's time in charge at Leeds was overshadowed by his office goldfish. Fans were outraged to learn that while there was no money for players, his pampered fish were having £20 a month lavished on them. Meanwhile, former Carlisle chief Michael Knighton claimed to have seen aliens on the M60 and Darlington FC owner George Reynolds has definitely seen a lot of things in his time – his previous employment includes stints as a thief, a safe-cracker and a bare-knuckle boxer.

SAY WHAT?

A fella hands over a £50 note to the turnstile operator at Upton Park and says, 'Two please.' The turnstile operator says, 'Will that be defenders or strikers?'

After scoring their 149th own goal, Stada Olympique heads were starting to drop

OWN GOALS

Sunderland's recent shipping of three own goals in one match might have been a Premiership record (one of many they broke in 2002/2003 – most consecutive defeats, that sort of thing) but they can take heart that it was a mere drop in the ocean compared to one team's efforts. Stada Olympique l'Emyrne of Madagascar scored a record 149 own goals in one match against champions Adema. The result was a protest against what they called 'partial refereeing', SOE repeatedly knocked the ball into their own net as the opposition looked on, bewildered.

ZIG ZAG ONION BAGS

Former Cambridge United boss John Beck has used some unusual motivational methods on his players in his time, such as encouraging them to chant the mantra 'zig zag onion bag!' before games. He also employed unique techniques on the opposition – treating visiting teams to over-heated dressing rooms, excessively sugary (or sometimes even salty) tea and balls soaked overnight in water to warm up with. Beck also ordered the Abbey Stadium groundsman to keep the grass long in the corners of the pitch to hold up his team's infamous long passes.

LAST MAN STANDING

The March 2002 Division One clash between Sheffield United and West Bromwich Albion is a strong contender for the most controversial game ever. Having slumped to 3-0 down with their goalkeeper and two substitutes sent off within minutes of each other, Blades manager Neil Warnock was accused by Albion's Gary Megson of deliberately trying to deplete his team in order to get the match called off. Two further Sheffield United players limped off with injuries, taking them down to six men which gave ref Eddie Wolstenholme no option but to abandon the match.

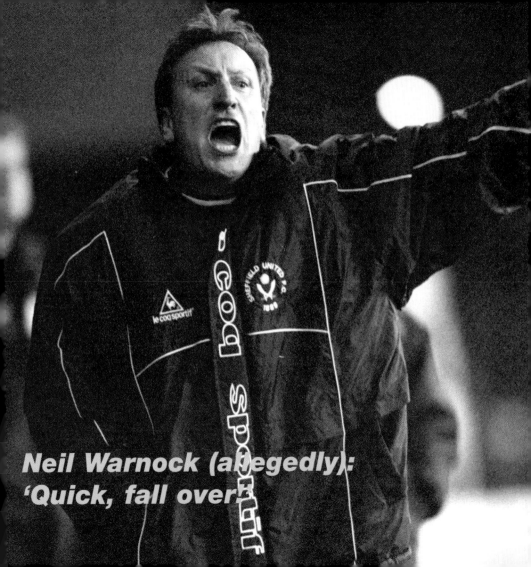

Neil Warnock (allegedly):
'Quick, fall over!'

THROW IN
THE TOWEL

Former Tranmere defender Dave Challinor was more famous for what he did with his hands off the pitch than with his feet on it. His long throw-ins were legendary and he made *The Guinness Book Of Records* for one 46-metre throw. To aid his throws, ball boys were issued with towels to dry the ball, and there were gaps in the perimeter fence with rubber mats on the ground to aid his run up. Opponents soon found ways to cramp his style. Bolton moved their advertising hoardings closer to the pitch to deny him a proper run-up and other clubs took to warming up their subs near to him.

Dave Challinor:
a threat to passing air traffic

ONE-SIDED GAME

The shortest game ever was the 1996 World Cup qualifier between Estonia and Scotland. The linesmen checked the nets, Billy Dodds passed the ball to John Collins... and the referee promptly blew for the end of the game. The reason was the absence of the Estonian team who stayed away in protest at Fifa bringing the kick-off time forward after Scotland complained about the quality of the ground's floodlights. Estonia even went through a reverse of the pantomime later in the afternoon, turning up at the stadium, switching on the contentious lights – hoping people would notice the difference – and pretending to be oblivious to the whole situation.

Scotland vs Estonia: 'Surely we cannae lose this one, lads!'

FLIPPING MARVELLOUS

Some people just don't know when to stop. While Peter Beagrie was the first English player to regularly celebrate scoring by executing a somersault, his efforts now look positively restrained. Newcastle's Lomano Lualua has managed as many as four flips to celebrate his goals for the Magpies but the undisputed master is Nigerian Julius Aghahowa. His 2002 goal to beat Algeria in the African Nations Cup might have been a tap-in, but the resultant celebration saw Aghahowa do six back flips and a somersault, taking him from the edge of the penalty area to the halfway line. Don't try it at home, kids!

HARD-BITTEN

Celebrating goals is no longer a solo pleasure; entire teams are getting in on the act. Some of the revelry is choreographed, of course – Aylesbury United FC achieved fame for their 11-man 'duck walk' across QPR's Loftus Road – but some definitely isn't. Unfortunate Seville striker Jose Antonio Reyes was engulfed by joyous team-mates when he scored in their 4-0 victory over Valladolid only for one, Francisco Gallardo, to take it too far. He pulled down Reyes' shorts and sunk his teeth into his penis. Gallardo, who blamed his team-mates for putting him up to it, was charged by the Spanish FA with infringing 'sporting dignity and decorum.'

LET'S ALL HAVE A DISCO

A holiday snap of veteran Irish striker Niall Quinn in some elaborate flares led to one of the strangest football chants of all time. 'They're better than Adam and The Ants/Niall Quinn's disco pants' has followed Quinn from Manchester City's Maine Road to Sunderland's Stadium of Light and was recently voted the funniest terrace chant of them all by fans. At least it isn't too personal. When Rangers' goalkeeper Andy Goram admitted his problems with schizophrenia, it didn't take long before Kilmarnock terrace wags struck up a chant of, 'There's only two Andy Gorams!'

FOOD FOR THOUGHT

We're used to continental managers bringing better dietary advice into the British game, but Cardiff City's Lebanese chairman Sam Hammam is getting a reputation for inflicting more exotic tastes on his players. At Wimbledon, he would punish defenders who conceded too many goals by forcing them to eat a portion of camel brains. And when he signed Englishman Spencer Prior for Cardiff City, Hammam slipped a clause into the contract saying that Prior had to eat sheep testicles. 'He is learning about Welsh people and sheep,' chuckled Sam. 'They have a horrible aftertaste,' groaned Prior.

It looks like an apple but it's really a sheep's testicle

IS THERE ANYBODY OUT THERE?

Goalkeepers are always barking orders to their fellow players, but sometimes, they can get detached from the action. In a non-league game between Witton Albion and Stocksbridge Steels, a goalie 'played' on for 10 minutes after the game was abandoned due to thick fog. Luckless keeper Richard Siddall couldn't see beyond his penalty area and assumed that all the action was at the other end. In fact, his fellow players were all huddled inside the dressing room. His manager Wayne Biggins eventually sent out a search party and found the puzzled player, literally, in a field of his own.

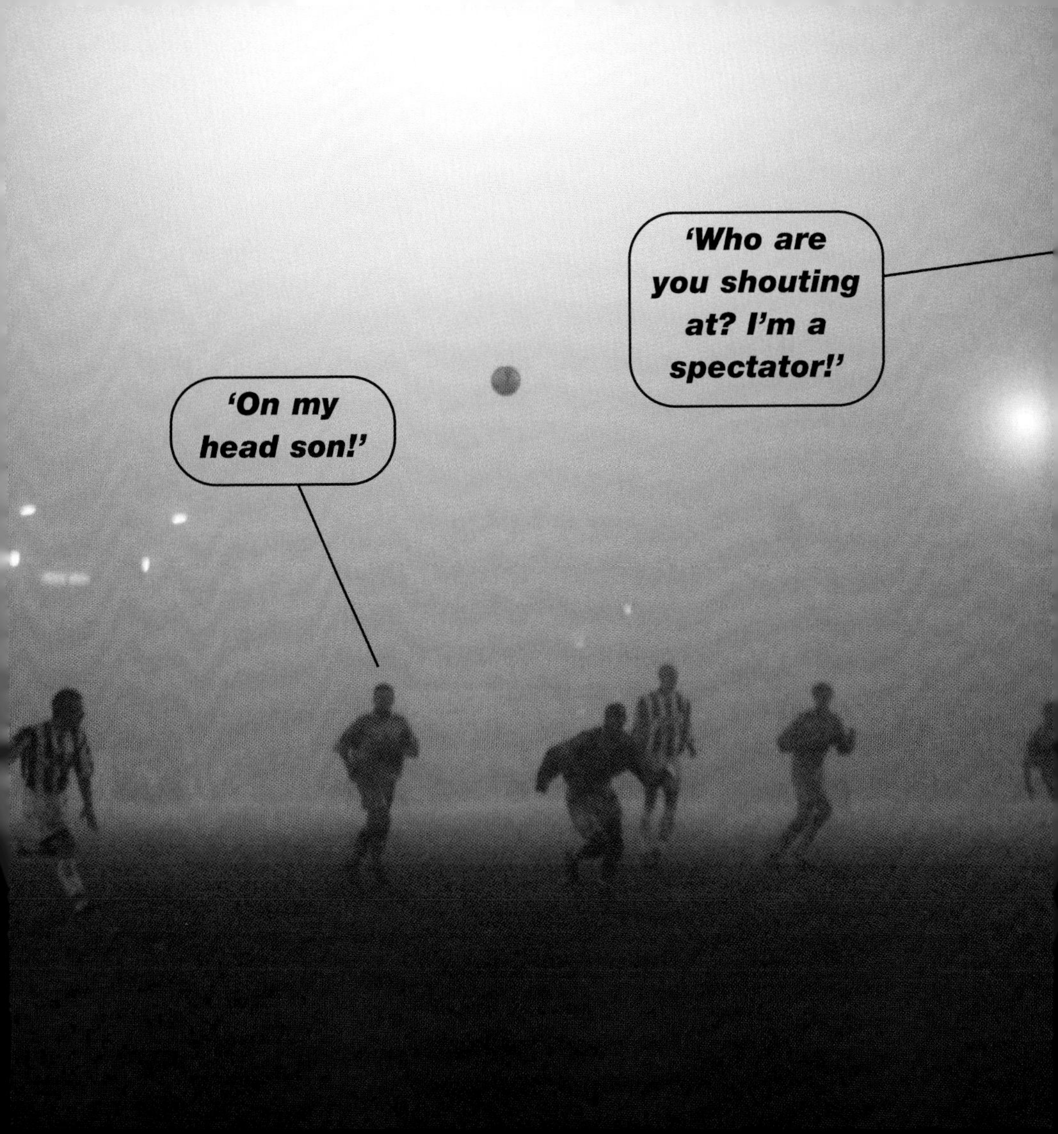
'Who are you shouting at? I'm a spectator!'
'On my head son!'

Transfer genius, Big Ron: smiling as he contemplates another shiny new lawnmower

SOMETHING FISHY

Although the most famous non-cash transfer in football was the set of tracksuits which bought the services of Tony Cascarino and 'Big' Ron Atkinson's claim to have once swapped a player for a lawnmower while managing non-league Kettering, they do things differently in Norway. Striker Kenneth Kristensen moved from Vindbjart to Floey, with the fee set as his weight in shrimp. The Floey directors are apparently very keen on fresh fish and Vindbjart agreed to bring a set of scales along the next time both teams met in order to weigh him.

VERY EARLY BATH

You might think that Taunton Sunday League striker Lee Todd's sending off after two seconds (for foul language after exclaiming 'That was f*****g loud!' when the referee blew his whistle) was the fastest ever. However, in 2002, Swansea City's Walter Boyd smashed that unwanted record. He came on as a substitute as the Swans were about to take a free-kick and immediately got himself involved in some nonsense in the box. The ref booked him, then after further dissent sent him off. Seeing as the free kick still hadn't been taken, that means technically Boyd was sent off after an unenviable 0 seconds.

'That's 10 you've sent off now, ref!'

TEMPER TEMPER

Dean Windass has a reputation as a combative player, but he's never likely to beat his 1997 record of attaining three red cards in one match while playing for Aberdeen. The omens weren't good – he was booked in the first minute – and eventually received his marching orders after 22 minutes. However, Dean didn't want to go, and a verbal blast to the referee earned another flash of the red card. When he eventually went towards the tunnel, it was via the corner flag, which he ripped out and threw to the ground. The ref scampered after him and carded him once more. Windass got a seven-week ban for his afternoon's misadventure. Perhaps he fancied a holiday.

NEWS AT 12

Penalty shoot-outs are the scourge of TV producers – with the evening news getting pushed back later and later. Usually decided after each side has taken five pens, it's still something of a rarity in the UK for a shoot-out to go to sudden death. But one Turkish cup match between Galatasaray and Genclerbirligi ended 17-16 on penalties and, amazingly, even that's not a record. During the 1980s when, to jazz up the game a bit, every match in the Argentine league ended with a penalty shoot-out, the strikers reached such frightening levels of competency that one game finished 20-19.

A WORD FROM OUR SPONSORS

The first team to feature a sponsor's name were non-leaguers Kettering, whose shirts advertised a tyre company. This was two years before the rules were relaxed, and the shirt was only used once (though ingenious Kettering tried to get around it, by changing their name to Kettering Tyres!). Nowadays every team except, famously, Barcelona carry sponsorship on their shirts. But did you ever wonder why Arsenal had two versions of their sponsor's ad, one featuring the word Sega, and the other emblazoned with Dreamcast? It came about after the Gunners realised that Sega is a rude word in Italian meaning 'an action of self love' (hint: it rhymes with bank).

Edit: along with the nation's football writers, praying the FA don't force him to put his full name on his shirt

WHAT'S IN A NAME?

For his first two games in the Premiership, Jimmy Floyd Hasselbaink ran out with 'Jimmy' on the back of his Leeds shirt. Eventually, FA killjoys ruled against such over-familiarity, fearing that every Tom, Dick and Juan Sebastian could follow suit (though the rules have since been bent by Edu). At least it was easy to spell. David Beckham turned out in the 1997 Charity Shield with his surname spelt 'Becham.' Not that he noticed. 'The players kept telling me my name was spelt wrong, but I thought it was wind-up,' he said.

German Burgos: perhaps the only goalkeeper to make the pages of Kerrang! And with hair like that, it's no wonder

STRIKING A CHORD

While plenty of rock and pop stars claim to have had trials as footballers (Rod Stewart at Brentford, Westlife's Nicky Byrne at Leeds, Steve Harris of Iron Maiden at West Ham) not many manage to combine the two careers. Except in Argentina, where the national team's goalkeeper, German Burgos, is a popular rock singer with two albums under his belt. His national team-mate, Barcelona left-back Juan Pablo Sorin, has had less luck, however. He was pictured in the papers dancing onstage with his favourite heavy metal group, Bersuit, the same day as he limped out of a training session with a mystery injury to his leg.

SAY WHAT?

Phil Neville is ill, so Alex Ferguson offers to go shopping for him. While in the local supermarket, he bumps into Arsene Wenger.
'Hello, Alex, what are you doing here?'
'I'm getting a sack of potatoes for Phil Neville.'
'Sounds like a fair swap to me!'

PIGGY IN THE MIDDLE

An Austrian FA Cup game between Wattens/Wacker and Saltzburg was held up for 20 minutes, not because of a dog on the pitch, but a pig! The 11,000 crowd cheered the porker's progress, as it wriggled free from no less than six hapless stewards. The animal refuge, which eventually took in the animal, reckoned that it was an escapee from a local butcher and suggested that, because of its 'lucky' status and sudden rise to fame, it would make a good club mascot. However, Wattens/Wacker's embarrassed head of security suggested it would make an even better sausage.

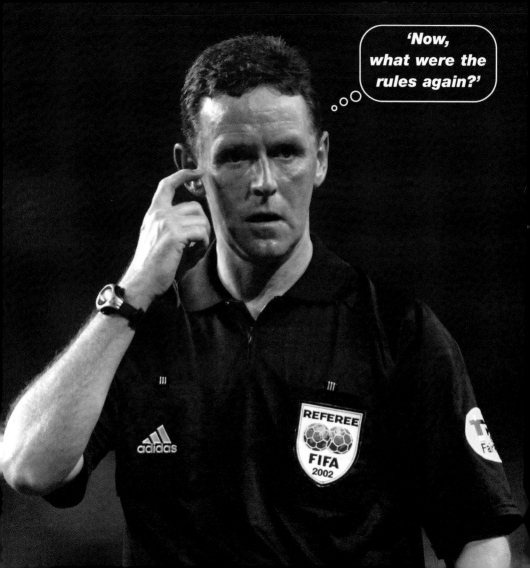

NOT OVER YET

The arcane rules of cup competitions can baffle fans and commentators alike – but you usually expect the referee to have some clue as to what's going on. However, when Witney Town equalised against Clevedon in the 112th minute of a Dr Marten's Cup game, all present – fans, players and referee – believed that the game was over, with Witney going through on the away goals rule. Wrong. Discussions between Clevedon's secretary and officials from the league revealed that away goals only counted double if scored in normal time. The jubilant Witney players were about to get on the team bus when a distinctly red-faced referee broke the news that they had to change back into their dirty kit, as the game was going to a late, late penalty shoot-out. Fortunately, they still won.

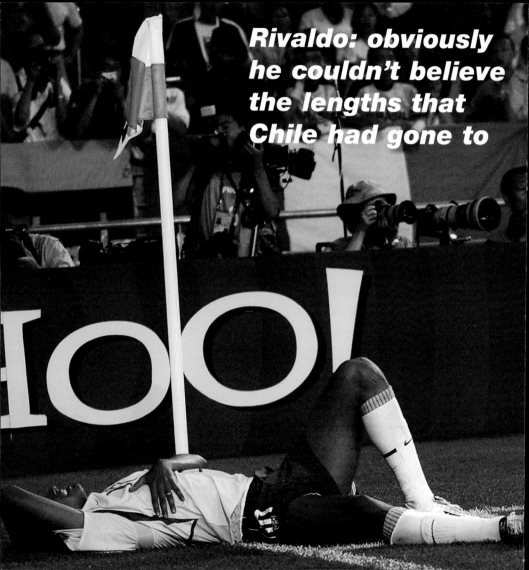

Rivaldo: obviously he couldn't believe the lengths that Chile had gone to

BLOODY MESS

The stakes couldn't be higher – a World Cup qualifier in front of 100,000 spectators; no wonder Fifa's general secretary suggested that Chile's actions in 1989 were 'the biggest swindle in the history of the World Cup.' With 20 minutes remaining and Chile facing elimination, goalkeeper Roberto Rojas fell to the ground clutching his bloodied face when a green flare was thrown from the crowd. Chile's players clumsily carried him towards the dugout where they stated that they couldn't continue the game as they feared for their lives. However, TV evidence later showed that the flare missed Rojas, who admitted to possession of a fake blood capsule. He was banned for life.

SAY WHAT?

A West Ham fan walks past a shop window and notices a video for sale entitled 'West Ham – The Glory Years.'
He asks the shopkeeper, 'how much for the video mate?'
'£200,' says the shopkeeper.
'£200 for a video?' says the Hammers fan, 'You're having a laugh.'
'Oh no,' the shopkeeper replies. 'The video's only a fiver, but that Betamax player's an antique.'

DOGGED DETERMINATION

Even the most persistent pitch-invading pooch rarely gets to do more than merely dribble with the ball or make a general nuisance of himself. Not so the mongrel who invaded the field of play during a Staffordshire Sunday Cup tie between Newcastle Town and Knave Of Clubs. A Knave striker in a one-on-one with the goalie took a shot at goal but sliced it. While everyone expected his effort to go well wide, they never banked on the intervention of Knave's four-legged friend who headed it past the keeper. The goal was allowed to stand, though the dog was never identifed and was therefore unable to pick up his win bonus. Or indeed Chum.

LET'S PLAY BALL

The referee's decision is final... unless it really annoys 22 players all psyched up for a game, not to mention a smattering of loyal fans. So when an evening reserve game between Norwich City and West Ham United was postponed due to a frozen pitch, angering all present who suspected that the ref didn't much fancy getting cold, they simply waited for the ref to leave, found themselves a replacement and played the game anyway. West Ham won 3-2.

DROPPED!

Celebrations can get out of hand at Arsenal. Sub Perry Groves once leapt from the bench and knocked himself unconscious on the roof of the dugout. Thierry Henry hit himself in the face with the corner flag and, after the 1993 League Cup Final, centre-half Tony Adams celebrated Steve Morrow's winning goal by lifting him onto his back. He lost his grip and unceremoniously flipped him over his shoulders and onto the Wembley turf, breaking his arm. Morrow was stretchered off with an oxygen mask over his face. The injury meant that he missed his chance to play in the FA Cup Final a few weeks later.

PRAISE BE!

Bolton Wanderers fans can thank divine intervention for their Premier League survival in the 2002/2003 season. With one match to go, St. Peter's Church hosted a sermon entitled 'What Would Jesus Say To Sam Allardyce?' There were humorous interjections from one churchgoer, dressed as the Wanderers boss and half-time oranges were passed around the parishioners. In the Argentinian city of Rosairo, meanwhile, they've gone one step further. A group calling themselves the Diegorian Brothers have set up a church dedicated to 'Hand Of God' star Maradona. Among their ten commandments is the instruction that all their followers should call their sons Diego.

Charlie Oatway: one of the biggest names in football

AND YOU ARE?

Many of our favourite football stars are working under assumed names. Nothing to do with foiling the taxman, of course, they've just opted to simplify their names a little. For example, Sol Campbell's real name is Sulzeer Jeremiah, John Lukic was really called Jovan and Jay Jay Okotcha was given the more prosaic real name of Austin. Others, like pundit Bob Primrose Wilson, try in vain to hide their embarrassing middle names from fellow pros. But there's no contest as to which player has the longest name. Brighton's Charlie Oatway was named after the 1970s QPR side, his full name being Anthony Philip David Terry Frank Donald Stanley Gerry Gordon Stephen James Oatway.

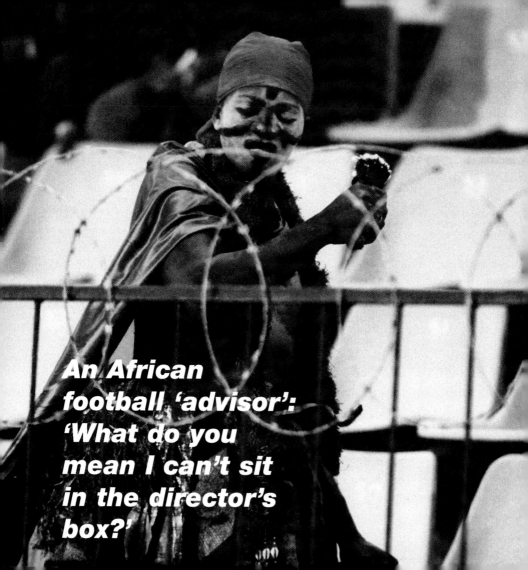

An African
football 'advisor':
'What do you
mean I can't sit
in the director's
box?'

THE WITCH REPORT

Eileen Drewery's spiritual advice to ex-England coach Glenn Hoddle was tame compared with the witchdoctors' influence in African football. Now officially banned, these dubious 'advisors,' known locally as juju men, used a variety of offbeat tactics to influence results. Kenyan side Gor Mahia were advised to smear themselves in pig fat before matches, avoid sex and choose a certain entrance to the stadium, lest their opponents had tampered with the main way in. After a run of bad form, a fox was exhumed in the centre circle of their pitch and they regularly used to place match balls in a grave overnight to harden them for the opposition.

SAY WHAT?

Peter Reid went to the Leeds halloween party as a pumpkin. Come midnight he still hadn't turned into a coach.

Fabien Barthez was
always a fan of Kojak
lollies as a child

THERE IS SUPERSTITION

During France '98 you can't have failed to have noticed defender Laurent Blanc taking time out to kiss the bald head of French goalkeeper Fabien Barthez before every game (even when Blanc was injured, he solemnly performed the ritual in his suit). Yes, footballers are a superstitious bunch and will stop at nothing to make sure everything is just so on matchdays. Paul Ince always puts his shirt on after he emerges from the tunnel, Teddy Sheringham always puts his right boot on first and Leeds manager Don Revie insisted on wearing the same lucky blue suit for ten years before all first team matches.

PLAY FOR TODAY

Now we know who wears the trousers in David Unsworth's house. His move to Aston Villa lasted only a week after his wife, who refused to move down to Birmingham, complained about his late returns from training to the family home. Villa manager John Gregory didn't help matters either, telling the papers, 'Apparently his dinner would end up in the bin.' When Norwich decided to release Ian Crook in 1996, he agreed to sign for local rivals Ipswich. He would wait until his Norwich contract expired to complete the formalities. However, when Mike Walker returned to Carrow Road as manager Crook still had one day left on his Norwich contract. Walker moved quickly and offered Crook a new contract as a coach – and Ipswich lost their man by a matter of hours.

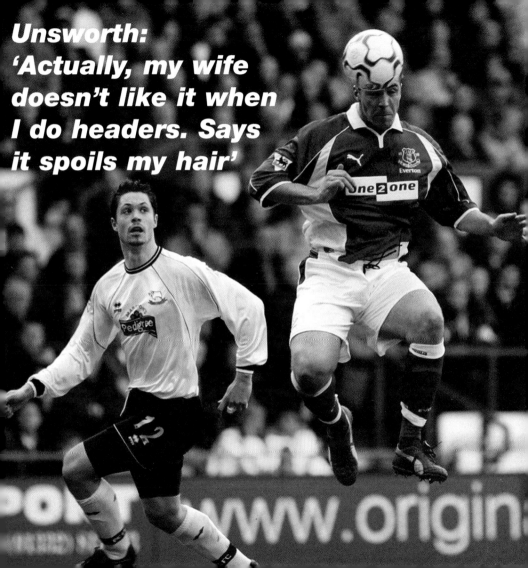

Unsworth:
'Actually, my wife doesn't like it when I do headers. Says it spoils my hair'

WOTCHA GHANA DO ABOUT IT?

The Ghanaian premier league's final relegation place was still up for grabs going into the last game of the season. With goal difference likely to come into play, there followed a bribery scandal of massive proportions. Both Brong Ahafo United and Hassacas bunged cash to their last-day opponents to get them to concede as many goals as possible and both benches kept in touch with events at their rivals' games by radio. By the end of the afternoon, Hassacas won 19-0 and Brong Ahafo won 21-0.

Another bribery scandal hits football in Ghana: 'They paid me a fortune to wear this!'

BOFFIN XI

Alastair McGowan's impression of David Beckham doesn't help, but footballers do have a reputation for being, well, a bit dim. There are exceptions: David Weatherall has a first in Chemistry and Bolton's Gudni Bergsson is a qualified lawyer who plans to practise in Iceland when he retires. And besides, Beckham might yet have the last laugh. Dr Keith Hanna, of software company Fluent Benelux reckons he has a stunning mastery of physics. He says that Beckham has figured out how to balance the kick angle, kick speed, spin imparted and kick direction to get the optimal turbulent-laminar transition trajectory for his free kicks. Well, that's easy for him to say.

TRUTH HURTS

When relegation is at stake, there's always some wag with a radio spreading misinformation. While he was in charge at Manchester City, that somebody was manager Alan Ball who, convinced that a 2-2 scoreline was enough to save the Citizens from the drop, ordered his players to play keep-ball. Unfortunately he got his sums wrong – City needed a win, and went down. Recently in Mexico, Atlético Colibríes fans were equally convinced that they'd beaten the drop. Even the players did a lap of honour. It took local journalists to break the news that actually results had gone against them and Atlético had been relegated.

MECHANICS OF THE GAME

Fukuoka, Japan was recently the venue for the RoboCup, attracting teams from 23 countries. However, unlike in television's *Robot Wars*, there are no remote controls: the robots are programmed to play a certain way and their creators can then only watch as the game unfolds. The RoboCup Federation aims to develop a robot team capable of beating the human World Cup holders by 2050. If that seems far-fetched, remember it only took 50 years for computers to beat humans at chess.

SAY WHAT?

Peter Reid is out shopping in town when he sees an old lady struggling with her shopping
Reid: 'Can you manage, love?'
Old Lady: 'Look, you took the job, you're stuck with it!'

Later play was held up due to a robot streaker

'So, we just play it through the channels': Another important Estonian cabinet meeting takes place

POLITICAL FOOTBALL

Though football has its supporters in the House of Commons and matches between politicians and the press are keenly fought, in Estonia, football and politics are inextricably linked. Toompea FC (which literally means Parliament FC) compete in the Estonian fourth division and one of their star players is Estonian Prime minister, Juhan Parts. Furthermore, he vies for a place in the team against his cabinet colleague the Minister for Justice, while the man in the tracksuit barking the orders at Toompea doubles up as secretary general of Estonia's Ministry of Defence.

FOOTBALL ROYALTY

Perhaps the oddest game of football in the world is the Royal Shrovetide Football game held annually in Ashbourne, Derbyshire. Contested between the up'ards and the down'ards (which side you're on depends on which side of the river you're born on), the match lasts for two days on a pitch that's three miles long. The only rule is that motor vehicles and manslaughter are banned. Well, obviously.

MASCOTS BEHAVING BADLY

Dundee's mascot Deewok the bear was assaulted outside the ground. However, his case didn't win much sympathy with the local police. His past comic exploits have included running onto the pitch with a flashing blue light strapped to his head, complete with matching truncheon and handcuffs, and he also got into trouble for shooting a policeman in the face with a water pistol and pretending to be drunk before a New Year's Day fixture. Deewok, who says his favourite song is 'Deewok' of Life by Dire Straits, has also raised a large amount of money for charity.

FRIDAY ON MY MIND

When Stockport County's manager noticed the side's only victories in one campaign had come on a Friday night, he opted to take the radical step of recreating night-time conditions at every subsequent fixture in a bid to trick the players' body clocks and to improve their flagging Division One campaign. The windows of the dressing room were blacked out, pre-match lunches were swapped for post-match dinners and the floodlights were put on at 3pm. It didn't help. They became the first team that season to be relegated, and finished bottom of the division.

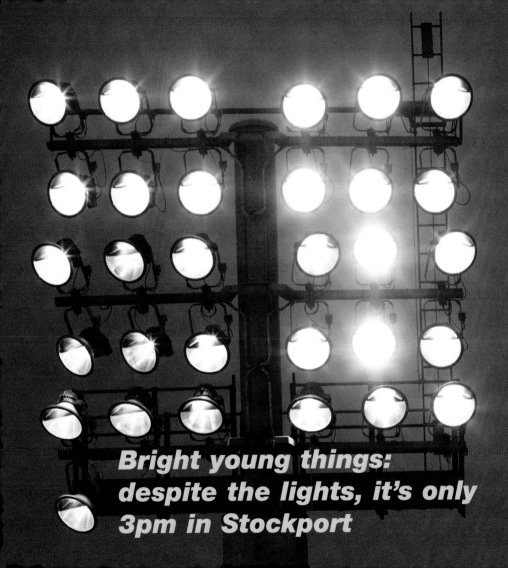

Bright young things:
despite the lights, it's only
3pm in Stockport

Shining light: Saint Bobby surveys the congregation at St. James's

IN BOB WE TRUST

A Newcastle United-supporting vicar spiced up his Sunday services by rewriting famous hymns in praise of Sir Bobby Robson. The Reverend Glyn Evans of St. Andrew's Church rewrote hymn lyrics to include 'Onward Bobby's soldiers,' 'All Things Black And Beautiful' and 'To Bob Be The Glory.' He said: 'If it means more people come together on a Sunday for worship, it's a good thing.' Visitors from nearby Sunderland might disagree.

SAY WHAT?

Q: Duncan McKenzie could jump over a mini, but which goal keeper can jump higher than a crossbar?
A: All of them, a crossbar can't jump!

WHAT PRICE LOYALTY?

Arsenal fan Mark Brewer might well be the unluckiest supporter ever. He spent £50 and two hours to get a tattoo of the club's crest etched on his left arm only for the Gunners to change the design a few days later. That followed on from his decision to name his three children – James Paul Merson, Matt Ian Wright and Holly Emmanuel Petit – after his favourite players, only for all of them to leave the club shortly afterwards. On the positive side, his family are walking Arsenal history.

NO SEX PLEASE, I'M A FOOTBALLER

It's accepted wisdom that footballers should avoid sex before matches. (Sex during matches is not such a great idea either). Most teams in the last World Cup practised a sex ban, though the Poles were an exception. Their generous coach allowed his players' wives to come over – provided that they paid their own air fares and stayed in a hotel 75 miles away from his squad. However Italian researchers at the University of L'Aquila reckon that sex before games actually benefits players. Their studies showed that levels of testosterone in men increase after sex.

The French demonstrate their new diversion tactics

THE WIT AND WISDOM OF...
RON ATKINSON

'The Bulgarian players are tried and trusted. Well, I'm not sure they can be trusted.'

'Zero-zero is a big score.'

'I would not say he (David Ginola) is the best left winger in the Premiership, but there are none better.'

'He dribbles a lot and the opposition don't like it – you can see it all over their faces.'

Big Ron
never takes
his eye off
the ball

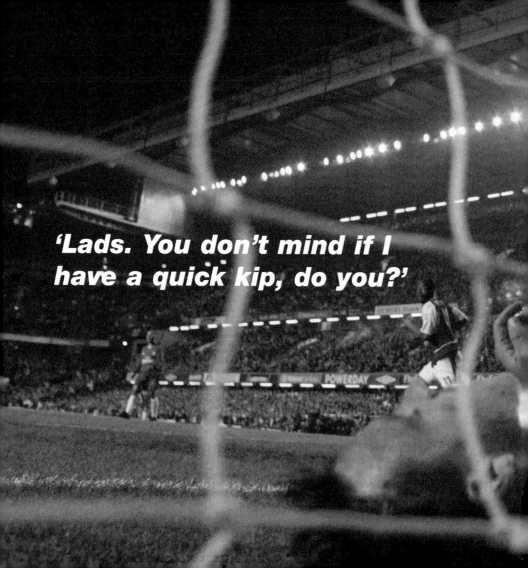

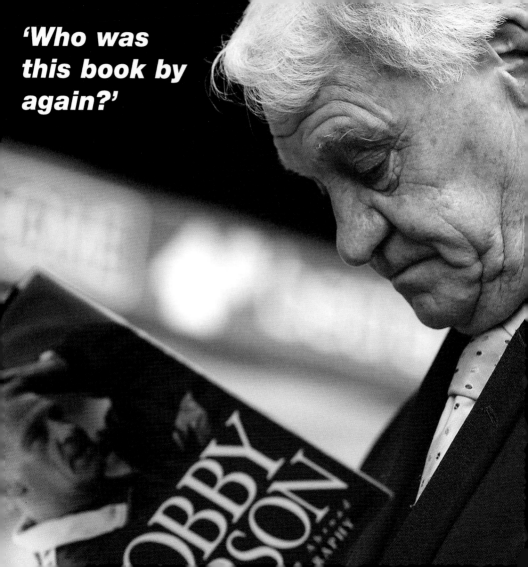

'Who was
this book by
again?'

THE WIT AND WISDOM OF...
SIR BOBBY ROBSON

'Look at that olive tree – 1,000 years old, from before the time of Christ.'

'He's very fast and if he gets a yard ahead of himself, no-one will be able to catch him.'

'I played cricket for my local village. It was 40 overs per side, and the team that had the most runs won. It was that sort of football.'

'I do want to play the short ball and I do want to play the long ball. I think long and short balls is what football is all about.'

THE WIT AND WISDOM OF...
GORDON STRACHAN

'I may get into trouble because I have been saying the two minutes of added time were up when the goal went in. If it was scored under two minutes I apologise to the ref for getting it wrong. If he's right then my watch is wrong and I'll ask him where he bought his from so I can get a better one.'

'If a Frenchman goes on about seagulls and sardines, he's a philosopher. I'd just be called a short Scottish bum talking crap.'

'I used to drive home from Manchester United training along the M56 and there was a left turn for Wilmslow, where I lived, and a right turn for Hale, where Norman Whiteside, Paul McGrath and Bryan Robson lived. I used to say that it was left for under three pints a night and right for more than ten.'

THE WIT AND WISDOM OF...
BRIAN CLOUGH

'Players lose you games, not tactics. There's so much crap talked about tactics by people who barely know how to win at dominoes.'

'I'm not saying I was the best manager in the business but I was in the top one.'

'He (David Beckham) should guide Posh in the direction of a singing coach because she's nowhere near as good at her job as her husband.'

'When the FA get into their stride they make the Mafia look like kindergarten material.'

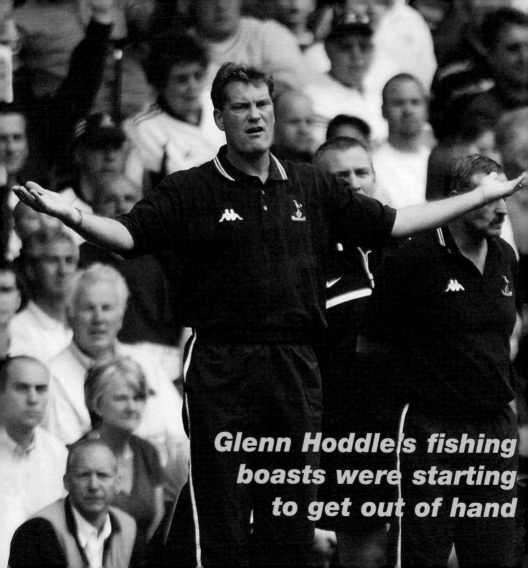

Glenn Hoddle's fishing boasts were starting to get out of hand

THE WIT AND WISDOM OF... GLENN HODDLE

'Michael Owen is a goalscorer – not a natural born one, that takes time.'

'OK, so we lost, but good things can come from it – negative and positive.'

'I think in international football you have to be able to handle the ball.'

'The minute's silence was immaculate, I have never heard a minute's silence like that.'

THE WIT AND WISDOM OF...
KEVIN KEEGAN

'England can end the millennium as it started – as the greatest football nation in the world.'

'You can't do better than go away from home and get a draw...'

'In some ways, cramp is worse than having a broken leg.'

'They're the second best team in the world, and there's no higher praise than that.'

'One day I'll learn to say no to my mum's home-made treacle toffee!'

El Tel reminds his team which way they're kicking

THE WIT AND WISDOM OF...
TERRY VENABLES

'They didn't change positions, they just moved the players around.'

'There are two ways of getting the ball. One is from your own team-mates, and that's the only way.'

'If you can't stand the heat in the dressing-room, get out of the kitchen.'

'It may have been going wide, but nevertheless it was a great shot on target.'

Author's Acknowledgements

Thanks to my girlfriend Liz Johnson for her patience as this project kept the football talk going well into the close season and to Al Harper, Nat Cramp, Roderick Easdale, Duncan Steer and Kathy Bal for their encouragement.

Picture credits

All pictures supplied by Getty Images

Essential Works

Design: Paul Collins and Colin Brown
Editorial: Roderick Easdale and Kelly Bishop
Picture Research: Allan Maxwell